AF525154

Contents

Foreword

This book took birth in my head on day one of our trip to the beautiful Andaman Islands. The place was sun-kissed and the company was a riot. Each moment spawned a story in my head. If I could have instantly downloaded everything as it happened, you would be holding a fairly large tome. Action-packed, laughter-filled, and with love and respect oozing for each other, this group of eleven women had such a wonderful time that the story begged to be shared.

In fact, Woodo, my woodpecker muse has been relentlessly pecking away at me since I got back from the trip. I could not take his torture and prickly sarcasm anymore. I put pen to paper, bent my head down, and turned this book around in record time to escape his torture. Woodo is now away on vacation to some distant lands.

This book is a celebration of the immense fun women can have if they manage to take a break from their somewhat self-imposed family constraints and responsibilities. When we go out and have the time of our lives, it is cathartic. We come back rejuvenated to pour even more love and care back into our families. It is a win, win!

Now it is up to you, readers, to enjoy this book, this labor of love, and draw inspiration to plan trips with your respective tribes. Go forth and have some fun!

1

The Beginning

It all started in the summer of 2019.

The boys said, "Let's meet for a drink." They met for a drink. They said, "Let's go on a monsoon-chasing trip." They went on a glorious three-day monsoon drive. They came back with tons of photos and many fun stories.

Their wives, the girls, were happy for them as wives tend to be. But secretly, they fumed. "How do these guys just up and away on their sojourns? Why can't we?"

This was a serious matter. It had to be discussed in depth. A clutch of girls met for dinner to dissect the subject and examine the entrails. The restaurant was Brahma Brews. Boy, did Brahma help us brew a mean brew!

That night, over dinner and drinks, a plot was hatched. We, the wives, would plan a trip to the Maldives. Yup! No local piddly one-day/two-day trip for us. We were going the whole nine yards. How we arrived at the Maldives as the destination is the stuff of a whole chapter in a different book. The Maldives was picked, plans were drawn, husbands were warned to stay home and take care of the kids, and we were off.

The Maldives was a fabulous three-day trip we couldn't stop talking about. COVID-19 came along and rained on any travel plans we tried to concoct after that. I suppose that was good in a way. We had raised the bar so high with the Maldives adventure that it was tough to plan another tour for fear it would not match up. In fact, at the end of the Maldives trip, one of the girls said, "Our next trip should be to nothing less than Bali or Hawaii, right girls? How can we settle for anything less?"

But the crowd was getting restless. We had tasted blood — freedom, I mean freedom. We were craving another 'all girls' vacay. It was taking over our mind space. Conversations on our WhatsApp group were dominated by "Where shall we go next?" and "When are we going?"

The decision-making process

The process was really simple. People just hurled whatever places they could think of into the WhatsApp group. Destinations ranged from Timbuktu to Waterloo, and from Kashmir to Kanyakumari. This went on for a bit while the girls engaged in several flights of fantasy.

At some point, we came to our senses and our discussions became more earnest and passionate. It was becoming clear that this group wanted a vacation urgently. We narrowed our list to beach destinations because no one wanted to wear the many layers of clothing required in cold climates. After that it was easy. Goa was too close by and too clichéd. Everyone and their aunts went to Goa all the time. The Andamans suggested itself by elimination and that was that.

I went out of town for a mere four days after that momentous decision was made. My WhatsApp blew up during that time. Who knew that the entire girl gang trip would be planned, approved, sealed, and signed off in record time? Before I could say '*whatchoo-all-doin*', a WhatsApp group was formed, a tour package was worked out, costs were agreed upon, and people had paid the initial amount. What? How? When? I had no time to ask any questions. I just closed my eyes and paid my share. The girl who had taken on the responsibility of organizing everything is *efficiency incarnate*. We believed our itinerary was in safe hands. She is the person I will address as Leader henceforth in this book.

Pro tip: For every girl gang trip, there has to be one designated leader. The rest of the gang must submit and emulate sheep. Where the leader goes, we simply follow. Ours not to reason why. Ours just to bleat and follow. There was one designated leader for the Maldives trip, too. It was a successful model. We simply replicated the process with a new leader. And boy, did she lead! It is not easy to herd ten wayward, 'head in the clouds' girls through a trip with a tight schedule. But Leader managed. We missed no sight and left no one behind! Her battle cry? *GIRRLLSSSSSS!*

That's all it took to round us all up over WhatsApp and everywhere on the trip.

2

Who Are We?

'We' refers to a strange cocktail of girls.

> *The Cambridge Dictionary defines 'girl' as a female child or young woman, especially one still at school.*

I was at school yesterday for my daughter's annual day. That should help me qualify as a girl, right?

Some would call us women. We'd rather not hear such references. We are girls, the female of the homo sapien species. Young, energetic, vibrant, full of life — yup, that's us.

For academic purposes and to satiate the insatiable curiosity of some of my readers, here is some data. We are in the age range of forty-two to fifty. Some of us turned fifty recently and don't want to acknowledge the fact. We are pleading deferral on reaching the age of fifty on the grounds that two years of the COVID-19 pandemic means everything was on pause, including aging.

How did such a mixed-age group get together, you ask? Are we colleagues? Did we meet at some cookery or dance class? At the local bhajan singing classes? Perhaps at a work-related conference?

None of the above. Now read carefully as I explain how we met.

The girls who are vociferously denying that they turned fifty are all classmates from school. That's about four of us in the group. The rest are the wives of the classmates of the four of us who turned fifty recently, hence the range of ages from forty-two to fifty. Some of the wives are so young, we had to contemplate whether they should even be allowed into our group of adults. We discuss all kinds of stuff within the group. Would the babies be able to handle it? As with any new generation, it turns out the youngsters know more. Never mind, then!

I am sure you are eager to know the names of the entire gang. Here goes:

Live Wire, who is full of energy, fast at everything, talks nineteen to the dozen, and is generally bursting with enthusiasm. She engages in 'no filter' conversations that provide unlimited entertainment.

Button, who is cute, well turned-out, dainty, and the phrase 'cute as a button' comes to mind when one sees her. She is also a compulsive gifter. She gave all of us a tiny pot of cold cream at the start of the trip, which came in handy for our chapped, sunburnt, and dehydrated lips.

Ms. Coach, who carries around a Coach® bag without the air of a person holding a Coach bag. The bag is infinite and contains anything that anyone needs. Mukhwas (mouth freshener), Dolo-650, candied fruits, chewing gum ... is that a bag or a bottomless pit? The bag reminded me of Hermione's bag in *Harry Potter and the Deathly Hallows*. The bag seemed capable of expanding magically while looking the same at all times. Coach® should consider signing her up as their brand ambassador.

Mom, who is considerate and thoughtful and always looking out for others. Some of the girls refer to her as Mom because she woke them, served coffee, and generally pampered them during previous trips. This time, I was a tad sick one night and Mom was on high alert. One cough from me and she was up rubbing my back and checking my temperature.

Pataki, or small firecracker, because she is quiet for the most part. Once in a while, she says something that makes the rest of us erupt in laughter. She kept up a steady supply of encouragement and convinced some of the girls to participate in seemingly scary activities. They reported that they had the time of their lives and thanked Pataki profusely.

Witty, because she is sharp and funny, and can wax eloquent about any topic. Constantly learning and seeking knowledge, Witty's other claim to fame is her ability to misplace mundane objects such as keys.

Earth Girl, because she reminds me of the phrase 'salt of the earth.' Quiet, observant, thoughtful, and helpful, she uses her words wisely and kindly. I observed her as much as I could while indulging in mob madness with the rest of the gang. She tries to leave as light a footprint on the earth as possible. I aspire to be like her when I grow up.

Diva of the group. Able to strike a pose in microseconds regardless of what she was doing just before that. At one point, she had a severe coughing bout. Someone whipped out a cell phone and pretended to click a picture. The cough was gone and she was ready with her pouty pose. She can go from sniffy and sick to striking a pose like a diva in a split second.

Princess, the dainty darling baby of the group, like a little cherub. Delicate in word and deed. She is the princess of the lot. Her eyes and hands have a conversation all by themselves when she talks. It is hard to focus on her words when we keep getting drawn to her shapely, manicured fingers that insist on having a separate conversation with us.

Leader, the designated leader for this trip who played her role to perfection. We all got home in one piece having seen all the sights we wanted to. The proof of the pudding. She became famous for her battle cry — *GIRRLLSSSSSS!* One cry from her, and we'd all assemble around her like sheep around their shepherd. There was no other way to round us up in a jiffy, and it worked like a charm, every time. This one time, some women from a neighboring group heeded her cry and huddled around too. That was the power of Leader's battle cry!

Writer, who would be me. I am writing this book, aren't I? I am open to a wittier name though. I am also *Muniamma*. You will read about why I was christened Muniamma later in the book.

Keep track of these names. Stay sharp. Form mental images of who is who, and fasten your seat belts as the ride begins!

3

Pre-planning

As the previous year ended and our trip dates got closer, the excitement of the group started mounting. Until a trip starts and ends as expected, there is some unmentioned tension in the air. Everyone is busy praying subconsciously for the trip's success. But that does not take away from discussions and preparations. When a group of this size is going on vacation, so many things need to be taken care of.

Shopping

The most important thing to plan was shopping. Where should we shop? What should we buy? A couple of simple rules were introduced early in the discussion, as we were heading to a beach destination.

- All clothes packed had to be above the knee. If anything was found to be below the knee, we had a couple of self-appointed Scissorhands who promised to snip away at the excess clothing.

- No piece of clothing should be big enough to be folded more than once. That's how skimpy and flimsy it had to be.

That's it. As long as everyone adhered to these two rules, packing was going to be a breeze.

Kaftan-kaftan

For our Maldives trip, we had gone shopping together and all of us bought red and white striped jumpsuits for the grand photoshoot. We called it the 'candy cane photo op.' It was quite a hit and we managed to turn heads at the resort we stayed at. Naturally, we were addicted to the adulation. We had to repeat the feat. What shall we do this time?

An idea germinated in my head. We were all definitely going to wear some form of swimwear at some point of the trip. Why not add a wispy kaftan on top and make that our photo shoot dress? Kaftans are totally in at this point and we are a bunch of fashionistas.

The idea was met with enthusiasm and put into action. Shopping together was impossible this time due to conflicting schedules. We improvised. We did not want the kaftans to look similar. So we mandated that each girl must post a picture of the kaftan they had ordered to prevent any repetition. The last thing we wanted was a sartorial faux pas.

Swimsuits

After the kaftan shopping brouhaha was done and dusted, we thought we were ready to pack and leave. Ha! Witty's mind was in motion. She waited till the last week to throw in a new idea.

Innocently, she asked, "Oh, by the way, are we not doing the thing we did for the Maldives?"

"What thing?" we asked.

"You know, where we wore similar dresses," she said.

"But we are doing kaftans instead of that," we said.

"Oh, but that was nice! We looked good," she said. That was all the incentive we needed.

The thing you have to understand about the psyche of a bunch of easily excitable women is that they will welcome every mad idea with enthusiasm; especially if the words 'dress' and 'photo' are used in the same sentence. In under two hours, we had hatched a plan to buy similar dresses. Leader and Princess went off to source said dresses.

This is how the whole thing fell into place. Witty wanted something similar to what we wore in the Maldives, but we did not want to buy another jumpsuit or a regular dress. The Maldives jumpsuits are rotting at the bottom of our cupboards after a single use. So we came up with the next best thing. Swimsuits! Yes, we decided to coordinate our swimsuits. A few pictures of Speedo swimsuits that could be passed off as dresses were shared on WhatsApp and the group arrived at a consensus.

You have to stop and appreciate this fact! A group of eleven women arriving at a consensus at record speed is a matter for the Guinness Book of World Records. There was a small hitch, though. Live Wire said she already had a similar swimsuit but in a different color. She was not too keen on buying another one. I thought that was darn sensible of her. I checked my cupboard. I seemed to have seven swimsuits. Seven! What have I been up to over the years? Fun fact — I cannot swim! This fun fact did not deter me from buying the new Speedo swimsuit for the Andamans trip. *Sensible* is not in my dictionary. As for Live Wire's predicament, no problemo. We had a solution. There were eleven of us. How perfectly odd! We'd put five on each side and make Live Wire the showstopper in all our photos. Why would she object to this brilliant plan? With that suggestion in place, the shopping spree started again.

Princess and Leader headed to a neighborhood shop for a reconnaissance mission. Was the color we selected available? What about sizes for all of us? We ranged from sub-zero to XXL. Everyone absolutely had to get their size. Also, how would the dress/swimsuit look when we wear it?

Leader and Princess tried on the swimsuits at the Speedo showroom and shared photos on our group. The rest of us were left salivating for our own — that's how good the swimsuit looked. We were running out of time to get our copies of this trip's fabulous costume.

4

Photomagnetism

Probably the most critical part of our entire agenda was the photo shoot. Scratch that. Make it plural. Photo *shoots* or photo *opportunities* were of extreme importance. It is rare to find such a large group of girls with such single-minded determination to click as many photos as possible. We were a motely crew on a mission.

In the build-up to the trip, some of the most exciting discussions were around possible ideas for group photos. Everyone shared photos from Instagram, Pinterest, and many other sources. Girls and women in beautiful poses brought out many *oohs* and *aahs* and expressions of 'we should totally do that' from the gang. Some of the photos shared included impossibly shapely young girls in impossible yoga poses. Such photos were immediately assigned to the two or three girls in our group who had a fair chance at assuming such poses. The rest of us promised to watch and admire.

Seriously, how are some women/girls so shapely, even after having a kid or two? I firmly believe such women should be declared illegal. How can it be allowed? How is it even possible?

Pro tip: When you plan a girl gang trip, make sure every member of the group is equally interested in photos — both posing for and taking photos. Your recruitment strategy for the girl gang must lend extreme importance to this aspect. It is a deal breaker. In our group of eleven, even if one of us had been photo averse, it would have rained on the parade. Every last one of us is photo crazy. We will pose for group photos and solos with equal enthusiasm.

The experiment

Very early in the trip, I conducted a mini experiment to test the photo readiness quotient of the group. At the airport, I grabbed one of the girls next to me, changed my camera to selfie mode, and pretended to click a picture. Another girl who was close by immediately inserted herself into the frame. Around here, we don't really have to stop and ask if it is okay to join in. I waited. In less than ten seconds, all eleven of us were wedged into the frame. Don't ask me how. There were no signals. No one called anyone. It was completely smooth.

I repeated this experiment a few more times because one cannot draw firm conclusions with a single piece of data. It worked the same way each time. In mere seconds, everyone inserted themselves into the frame. Others adjusted their positions to fit the new person in and we were group-photo ready with military precision.

My experiment had been deemed successful. Someday I will write a full thesis about this phenomenon. Here is the summary for the academically inclined:

Our phone cameras are magnets, especially for certain girl gangs. Someone needs to just whip out the phone and switch to selfie mode, and all eleven of us gravitate without our knowledge toward the camera. I am not kidding. It happened throughout the trip, unfailingly.

You can use this trick to check if everyone in your girl gang is photomagnetic, too. It is also a great way to gather the masses when it is time to head back. Just bring out your camera and switch it to selfie mode. That's it. Watch the girls gather.

In the plant kingdom, plants that gravitate toward sunlight are supposed to display positive phototropism — think sunflowers.

> In our girl gang kingdom, we all display *positive cameratropism* — we are attracted to cameras.

Photo shoot idea line up

The enthusiasm and diligence with which photo ideas were shared within the group might have led an innocent bystander to believe that photos were the sole goal of this trip. Maybe we were celebrities, and this was our Kingfisher Swimsuit Calendar assignment. In our heads, we were important enough to commission our own swimsuit calendar. Why not?

Many photo ideas were shared, upvoted, or downvoted in preparation for our big photo shoot operation. With so many ideas already in our heads, we were ready to face the camera.

5

What Should We Pack?

Several reams of paper were dedicated to the topic *what do we need to pack*? Everyone had doubts. Questions were asked and answered on the WhatsApp group.

Should we carry beach towels?

No. Carry ordinary towels. Enough.

How many pieces of footwear should we carry? What kind of footwear to carry?

Three. Shoes for the flight. Fancy heels for dinner. Flip flops for the beach. Button brought several pairs to match various dresses. We do not know how her luggage was able to fit all this and stay under the luggage limit. An unsolved mystery.

What will we wear on which day?

Who knows.

How many times do we need to change clothes during a single day?

At least thrice. Morning, after visiting the beach, and for dinner. And then into night clothes as well. So maybe four times?

When is the kaftan photo shoot?

Maybe day two? Maybe day three? Don't know.

When is the swimsuit photo shoot?

Maybe day two? Maybe day three? Don't know.

Will we be able to wash our clothes?

Ayyo! Where is the time?

How will we carry our wet clothes from one place to the other?

In plastic bags. But they will dry fast. It is hot out there.

On which day will we wear our fancy and blingy dinner dress?

Bring two or three fancy dresses. We will dress for dinner each night.

Who is bringing accessories?

Me, me, me, me (in short, almost everyone).

What SPF value of sunscreen do we need to buy?

This was one of the longest and most confusing conversations.
It has to be more than SPF 60. I bought this one - see attached photo. Mine is SPF 75. I have SPF 30, I will adjust with that.

Types of packers

When there are eleven people, you have to accept that there will be several styles of packers:

- The one that packs a week in advance, makes sure every little piece of clothing including lingerie is ironed and folded in clear plastic bags. People were aghast that she did not have a cover for her suitcase this time.

- The one that weighs and re-weighs the luggage repeatedly to ensure the luggage limit of the flight is not exceeded. She also announced the weight at regular intervals, causing others to panic and weigh their luggage and re-pack. It was a vicious cycle.

- The one who keeps repeating that she has not started packing and will only pack at the last possible minute but turns up with all the right clothes and accessories anyway.

- The one who tried all her clothes, found they didn't fit, went on a shopping spree, and bought a whole new set of clothes for the trip.

- The one who runs a company, finished packing within one evening, and managed to make yummy sweets to feed us all during the trip. I think she has forty-eight hours a day. She is just refusing to admit it!

- The one who said nothing, kept quiet through it all, brought one cute piece of luggage and managed to coordinate her earrings, neck pieces, footwear, nail polish, and everything else with minimal fuss.

- The one who made her own checklists,

systematically packed everything a few days ahead of time, made her husband check once to ensure nothing was forgotten, and never found a single thing during the trip. She had to keep borrowing stuff from others. Sheesh!

- The one who packed for herself as well as for the rest of us. She had an endless supply of anything anyone wanted. Extra clothes, scarves, hats, moisturizer ... you name it, she had it.
- The one who claimed she needed advice but packed efficiently, troubled no one, and seemed to have everything she needed at the right place and at the right time.
- The one who packed various necessities as well as a big hat because beach destinations are incomplete without big hats.
- The one who packed on the last day with the speed of quicksilver and even made a handy ready reckoner for others:

Packing list

Dresses
Make-up kit
Medicines
Toiletries
Purse
Backpack
Towels
Swimsuit
Sunglasses
Lingerie
Hat
Scarf
Kaftan
Phone
Charger
Power bank
Money
Credit card
Ticket
Identity proof
Pads
Plastic bags
Water bottle

The others squealed in audible delight when they saw the checklist. The squealing echoed all over our WhatsApp group. This was great! We quickly checked off everything on the list and felt happy that were indeed ready for the trip.

Here's a task for you, my reader. Match the packers with the personas!

Luggage limit brouhaha

Things cannot be simple, right? Just as we were getting complacent about everything and everyone being ready, Mom dropped a bomb on us.

Before I explain the devastating bomb, I have to give you some information. Our flight tickets were booked in two batches. We had two onward and two return tickets with an assortment of us attached to each ticket. Ticket one for the onward journey had six of us listed on it and ticket two had the other five listed on it, and so forth.

Mom and some of us were listed on one ticket. Mom noted on the group that the luggage limit for the onward flight was 75 kgs and the limit for the return was 90 kgs. She was ecstatic — these airline guys must know about our shopaholism! They had given us leeway to carry extra luggage on the return flight, she opined. There was an excited buzz on the group while each of us dreamed of all the things we would shop for.

A couple of minutes later, Mom was back. She said she was confused. Actually, the onward limit was 90 kgs and the return was 75 kgs. *What*? We were gobsmacked. Some girls began to panic. Live Wire was terribly upset. She had finally finished packing at the end of her hectic workday.

"Wet clothes will weigh more. What are we supposed to do with such a low luggage limit?" she exclaimed.

I was perplexed. Which airline increases or decreases the luggage limit like this on a single destination flight? I checked our tickets carefully. Aha! Each of us had a 15 kg individual luggage limit.

On the onward ticket, there were five of us listed.

15X5 = 75 kgs

On the return ticket, there were six of us listed.

15x6 = 90 kgs

Math complete.

I said, "Hey Mom, er Mom? See the number of people on the return ticket." I said this hesitantly because Mom is not prone to such mistakes.

Silence.

Then Mom said something unbelievable.

"Busted!! I finished packing and am all set. I was bored. I thought I'd introduce a worm in your collective heads and have some fun. Hahahahahaha!"

Live Wire was not amused. She unleashed a bunch of unmentionable expletives at Mom. I dropped my phone because WhatsApp turned red! It was hilarious! What a smooth scammer Mom turned out to be!

6

At the Airport

D-day! After months of anticipation, the day of our departure dawned bright and clear. We had to pinch ourselves to make sure this was happening. Having gone through weeks and weeks of waiting and talking about the upcoming trip, and being afraid of jinxing it, we were actually headed to the airport. Gosh!

Will we? Won't we?

I had a minor concern. When I finally checked the onward air ticket and noted the airline, I remembered a news item from just about a week ago. We were flying on an airline that was in the news for all the wrong reasons. This airline had left fifty-four people on the tarmac and gone on to its destination. What was their hurry? Those fifty-four people had been on a bus heading towards the plane when they suddenly found themselves waving their flight goodbye. The news item went on to explain that the airline owned up to its mistake and flew those hapless passengers to their destination on the next flight. Nonetheless, it was worrisome to note we were booked on that very airline. Imagine eleven of us being stranded on the tarmac. Worse, what if five of us made it to the plane and six of us were left behind, or some such combination? Imagine if Leader was one of those left behind on the tarmac. Disastrous. The rest of us would be left bleating because we had no clue where to go, whom to contact, or anything else. Leader was our only hope and beacon of light!

Luckily, no such drama occurred. We all went on the trip, had an amazing time, and I am here to tell the tales. *Tales*. Yes. So much to report from a mere five-day trip!

Cab pooling

The good news is that all of us live in and around South Bangalore. It was easy to work out cab pooling options to get to the airport.

Ms. Coach, Pataki, and I were scheduled to go in a pooled cab from my area. We met on the dot at the appointed time. But others were already on their way. Worse — they posted photos of themselves in their cab. Oh, the pressure of competing with eager beavers heading early to catch the same flight we were trying to get on! We posted our photo too, but we had lost the race of 'who will post their *airport look* photo first.'

One group was so eager that they could not wait outside for the herds to gather. Those five early birds went right into the airport, checked in, and started posting photos from the VIP lounge to which they had access. Show offs! Hmph! What happened to the 'all for one and one for all' sentiment I wonder!

The rest of us were patient. We waited for each other and went in together. We *chose* to eat like common citizens at the regular eatery. No fancy VIP lounges for us. Actually, we were very hungry and just wanted to eat. We could not find the entrance to the lounge. Don't tell the other five.

We got male

The queue to obtain our boarding pass was long. Murphy's Laws were in action causing us to be stuck behind the line that refused to move. We were standing around complaining about how long it was taking when one of the girls spotted another counter with an airline official behind it. But there was no one in line trying to check in at that counter. She wondered why. Almost at once, she figured out the reason and explained it to us. The board above his head said 'Male.' None of us qualified. Hence we could not access that counter. Right? We waited for a few seconds to see if she would realize that her conclusion was wrong. Nope. She was convinced. We almost didn't want to break her illusion. But then, we were bursting with giggles. We had to tell her. *Male* in this case was not the gender. It was a destination. Malé is the capital of the Maldives.

You should have seen her face when comprehension dawned on her! The rest of us howled with laughter. Thus began a trip filled with many such crazy moments that will last in our collective memories for a lifetime.

Up, up, and away

After our boarding passes were obtained, the next agenda was obviously foraging for food. What is it about trips? At home, on a normal day, we can go without breakfast till late in the morning. Step out on a journey and we feel hungry at once, no matter what time of day it is. We were ravenous. Have you ever tried to order food as part of a large group? It is almost akin to a mission impossible. If only Tom Cruise could come along and sort it all out. Actually, I doubt Tom Cruise, with all his talent, can handle this challenge. Finally, Mom took charge, somehow managed to remember everyone's orders, and brought us our food. It was like a mamma bird coming back to the nest with worms in her mouth while the baby birds jumped up and down and squawked, trying to get all the worms into their gawking mouths. What a ruckus we created! The five lounge birds also joined in for good measure. Luckily, they were well-fed and had no interest in the food. The downside though was that their mouths were free to chatter. They participated in the ruckus-making with extra energy. I don't know if the airport café had ever witnessed this level of a cacophony!

Despite being an unruly and raucous group, we managed to reach the airport and get our security clearance done without a single hitch. We were seated near the boarding gate well ahead of time. Then we waited and waited ... and waited. Almost everyone around us left, but our flight boarding was not announced. Finally, Live Wire, who clearly had a wee bit of her wits about her, went to the neighboring gate to check. Guess what? They were announcing the final boarding call for — hold your breath — *our flight*! We were apparently waiting at the wrong gate! Gosh!

Pink-faced with embarrassment, we rushed towards the gate and boarded the bus that would take us to the waiting aircraft. We did not have time to check who among us had announced the wrong boarding gate and give them some choice words. We just about made it to our seats. For some time, there was a real danger of us being left behind on the tarmac for no fault of the airline.

My wise mom used to quote this often in Kannada — *maathu mane haalu maadthu*. This loosely translates into 'talking will ruin our homes.' When we start chattering, we lose track of everything. Funny how none of us thought to check why our boarding was not being announced.

Love thy neighbor

We are an excitable bunch. We can get excited about just about anything. When we completed our web check-in, we realized that one of us would sit next to a stranger. Eleven girls seated three in a row meant we had four rows to ourselves, except for one seat. The one with the seat next to the stranger was suddenly the object of great attention from all of us. We were like giddy teenagers. Who would sit in seat 9C? Male? Young? Handsome? While we speculated, it was easy to forget that we were not young. We only remembered these wise words:

> *A thing of beauty is a joy forever.*
>
> John Keats

With that thought in mind, we were hoping for some eye candy during our short trip. Call us greedy, no problem.

9C turned out to be a reasonably young and good-looking man. But when we finally settled into our seats, we reverted to our true selves, cast our eyes down, and behaved decently. In other words, we got totally caught up in our own chatter, ordering food, teasing each other, and such internal matters. That's another thing about girl gangs. We are self-sufficient. We do not need external stimuli for fun. We have enough nonsense going on amongst us that we have no time to look outside.

7

The Overloaded Itinerary

No one looked at the itinerary that Leader sent us. We are sheep. We just follow.

But sheep apparently wake up in the nth hour. We understood that it was to be a four-night/five-day trip. Good. The duration was just perfect. We checked the program and panicked. There was way too much action. Our 'always ready to panic' minds could not fathom how we would cover all this and manage to pack and change and unpack and re-pack through it all.

Looking at the schedule left us a bit breathless.

Pro tip: If you are planning a trip with your girl gang, do take the time to peruse the daily schedule in advance. See if you can cut down on some activities, prune the schedule a bit, and so on. Or leave it all to the trip leader and indulge in a shot of *que sera sera*. Whatever will be, will be. We did just that and it all worked out fine.

Day 1: Bangalore to Port Blair by a 2.5-hour flight

- Evening at Port Blair

Day 2: Port Blair to Havelock Island by ferry

- Elephant Beach
- Radhanagar Beach
- Havelock Island Resort for the night

Day 3: Neil Island by ferry

- Bharatpur Beach
- Natural Bridge
- Sunset at Laxmanpur Beach
- TSG Aura Resort for the night
- Sunrise at TSG Aura

Day 4: Port Blair

- Cellular Jail
- Ross Island
- Birthday party and dinner (sshh! The birthday party is a secret)

Day 5: Port Blair to Bangalore

- Shopping
- Leave for the airport
- Arrive in Bangalore tanned and tired

In hindsight, this was a good itinerary. We could have potentially cut down a place or two, but at the time it seemed right. We did not rush through any of the spots planned. Everything was well-planned and timed to perfection. We kept time. There were no delays because of us. We are pros, apparently.

8

Port Blair

We arrived at Port Blair and were whisked off to the hotel in a Tempo Traveller. Eleven girls, eleven suitcases, an odd assortment of handbags, a large bag full of hats, and non-stop chatter were tipped onto the sidewalk in front of our hotel. We were eager to get into our rooms and freshen up.

We were eleven. We had five rooms. This was now a math puzzle. One of us would have to be split into five and distributed equally among various rooms. That seemed a bit harsh on that one person. Instead of one of us taking this burden, three of us volunteered to share a room for all four nights we were going to spend in various hotels across the Andamans. We did not ask for an extra bed — instead, we just squeezed into one bed. This naturally led to a lot of innuendo-filled chatter for the rest of the trip. Three people? One bed? Snicker snicker! To those who did not join us on the trip, we can only say, "What happens in the Andamans stays in the Andamans!"

We were allotted rooms next to each other on the third floor. Everyone got busy finding rooms and partners and things like that. Mom, Witty, and I, who were going to share a room, received our key. Witty went off to get our luggage during which she missed some important happenings.

I opened the door to our room and laughed. I said, "How cute, they already laid out our bathroom slippers for us." There was only one pair laid out. That did not strike me as odd at all. Mom, who entered after me, did not laugh. She is clearly more observant and thoughtful. She said, "There are clothes on the bed too. This does not look right." Wait, what? Did they lay out clothes for us. Would any hotel go to such an extent? My mind was engulfed in a fog. Mom was cleverer though. She guessed that the room was already occupied. In fact, our room looked *preoccupied*, just like our minds were at that point! We rushed back to the hotel reception. The guy at the reception refused to believe us. He felt someone in our group might have gone in ahead of us. His face wore an expression that said, *these big groups of women are clueless, sheesh*. Really, Mister? Do you think we are *that* scatterbrained? I mean, he *did* have a point. We were *capable* of it, but not this time. He had given me the key just two minutes ago. I went straight to the room and opened the door. The key had never changed hands. There had to be an explanation for the appearance of clothes and footwear in a fresh room assigned to us.

After much back and forth, the hotel folks decided to investigate. I don't know what they found or who the clothes belonged to, but we were given a different room. This was the start of many unsolved mysteries on this trip. Mom and I shuddered at the thought that we could have potentially walked in on all kinds of action in the room. The clothes were there. Where were the owners? And what were they wearing? Good thing we did not open the bathroom door. Whew! Escaped by a whisker.

After the dust settled on this strange commotion, we ordered lunch at the restaurant and got ready for our evening out in Port Blair. Some parts of the original itinerary had to be canceled because of restrictions related to VIP movement in Port Blair, but that did nothing to reduce how much fun we milked from whatever else we did that evening.

Let me digress a bit to tell you about the lunch ordering procedure. When there are eleven girls in various stages of getting ready for an evening on the town, ordering lunch can go out of control pretty fast. After that, there is not much time for an evening around town or anything else for that matter.

Pro tip: When ordering lunch or dinner for a big group, hand total control over to one person, or two, at max. Trust them to make the right choices, and then proceed to quietly eat whatever they ordered. If you are unhappy with their choices, take over the reins the next time.

In our case, two of us marched down to the restaurant, grabbed hold of a passing waiter, and asked him what could be delivered fastest to our table when the crowds descended. The startled waiter had to restart his brain before he could give us a coherent response. I don't think he is used to being grabbed mid-stride, especially by two women who look like they mean business. We understood that phulkas, mixed veg curry, and jeera rice could arrive quickly. We did rapid math and told him how many phulkas, bowls of curry, and plates of jeera rice he needed to bring to our table in under fifteen minutes. As the prettily dressed and babbling girls arrived at our table, the food arrived too. We were able to finish and leave in record time.

Promenade Road

A twelve-seater cab arrived, we packed ourselves into it, and the cab shot off towards promenade road. The van driver dropped us at the far end of the road, advised us to just walk back along the same path, and call him when we were ready to head home. Good plan, yes. Except, when you offload eleven girls who are dressed to the nines, walking even a hundred yards without stopping for selfies is a bit of a tall order.

We found that our legs were made of lead. We simply could not move beyond a few steps. The promenade road along the sea was beautiful. It was a well-lit stretch with a parapet to sit on and stare out into the sea. We could hear the waves crashing gently against the wall. We stood here. We stood there. We clicked group photos and solo photos. We checked for better lighting. We grabbed other tourists to click our photos. No other visitor looked that busy on that road.

Finally, when we could not click any more photos, we spotted a chai wallah (tea seller). He was mobbed immediately. The guy was unfazed. He had the resigned air of one who has seen it all. He served us piping hot tea and told us to gather all the paper cups in one place. "Don't throw the cups into the ocean," he warned. We dutifully gathered the paper cups in a corner and the chai wallah materialized to collect them. Wow! We felt so proud of how well the city is regulated. The entire walkway was spotless and we enjoyed a long stroll after re-energizing ourselves with hot chai.

Meanwhile, our tour operator apparated out of thin air and called us over to explain the itinerary to us. Within two minutes, he lost half his audience to bhel puri. After some time he lost a few more girls to cut raw mangos smeared with salt and chilly powder. He is now undergoing therapy because he cannot compete with bhel puri and raw mangos. The tour guy really should not take this personally. Raw mango has raw magnetism. No one can resist its charms. Only a couple of us were left behind to listen to him. I was one of them, but I was doing everything in my willpower to prevent drool from leaking out of the sides of my mouth as I watched the other girls hogging delicious street food. I don't know if anyone heard anything he said.

In fact, I vaguely remember him saying something about not missing the night sky at Neil Island. I believe he said we can see the Milky Way on a clear night. Some part of my brain did perk up at that point. But that part was quickly drowned under the flood of saliva caused by huge billboards of raw mango being erected in other parts of my brain. I did not remember about the night sky until after we left Neil Island. When at Neil Island, we congregated in one room and spent the night chattering. We could have done that outside, looking up at the sky, starry-eyed. But who remembered that piece of information? The Milky Way! Dash it all! What a missed opportunity!

Back on Promenade road, at the end of an hour-long windswept walk where we caught up with each other, swapped stories, and discussed life, we were ready to head back to our hotel. The van driver was summoned and we trooped in. By this time, the fruitaholics of the group were in action. We spotted a row of fruit stalls with a beautifully arranged assortment of local fruits. The van floor was suddenly awash with drool. The driver had to execute an emergency stop to prevent the fruitaholics from bursting out of the van through the windows. Bagloads of fruits were bought. Several hands and mouths appeared. In a short while, the pile of fruits was reduced to mere skin and seeds. Never have I ever seen so much fruit-o-mania. This was repeated at regular intervals throughout the trip.

What a fruit frenzy sight
When fruitaholics of the world unite!

Anu Anniah

9

Off to Havelock Island

On day two, we rose at the crack of dawn, brushed, finished other unavoidable morning activities, changed, and were at the Port Blair hotel reception by 5:30 am. We had to catch an early-morning ferry to Havelock Island. There was much to see and do and no time to be wasted. We clicked several essential selfies while we waited for the van that was to take us to the ferry point.

A packed breakfast was ready for us at the hotel reception. All we had to do was pick up one box each and head out. For some reason, that was a very complicated task. There was so much chaos. We took a good ten minutes to sort it all out and ensure everyone had one and only one box each. We are not greedy, just overzealous. In a fit of consideration, some girls picked up their roommates' breakfast boxes in addition to their own leading to widespread mayhem and confusion. It is hard to explain how something this simple can get so chaotic in such a short time.

On the ferry

As a general rule, woe betide anyone else who happens to be on the same plane, bus, train, hotel, dinner table, or even beach as a bunch of excited girls out to have fun. It is not that we have no regard for others. We just stop seeing anything or anyone else. It is as if the entire world is available to us and everyone else has vaporized for those few days. If you are out to have a quiet time somewhere and see a big girl gang, I would advise you to leave and find someplace else.

We settled into our seats on the ferry and stared quietly out at the great blue sea from the huge windows. We ordered chai from the in-house service as we bobbed along peacefully. Then the crew made a mistake. They played music. Not just any music. *Bollywood* music. Some of us started quivering involuntarily in our seats. The crew made the biggest mistake after that. They invited people to the dance floor. That was all we needed. A small nudge. We had no time to waste. Who knew how much longer the journey was going to last? We had so much dance trapped in our collective selves — it had to be unleashed. The rest of the hapless passengers just sat there gawking while we huddled on the tiny dance floor, danced, collected more folks from among the other passengers, ran around in circles, shouted, laughed, and had the time of our lives. Being part of a big gang is liberating in so many ways!

We set the ferry's dance floor on fire. Although music and dance must be a regular feature on their trips, I suspect they had never seen such a motivated group of dancers earlier. We danced as if our lives depended on it. The ferry staff watched us agog. One of them joined in and even taught us some of her local dance steps. It was a riot.

The crew handed us a cap each and said they were exclusively for us, since we had started dancing first. We were blown away. To show our gratitude and also because a really nice dance number started playing, we danced with renewed enthusiasm. Later, we saw the crew giving away caps to everyone. Cheaters! Enchiladas! Oh, well, we had our moment in the spotlight.

When the music stopped, we had way too much adrenaline coursing through our bloodstream. We filed back to our seats, over-excited, unable to contain our chattering or volume. Too bad, neighbors. Maybe we should carry earplugs and hand them out next time. We can't behave ourselves, but we *can* help others retain their peace and sanity.

No elephants on Elephant Beach

We disembarked from our dancing ferry, walked some distance, watched our luggage being loaded into a van, packed ourselves into another van, and embarked on another short boat ride. We reached Elephant Beach.

No, it wasn't that simple. There was lots of confusion about the day's program. Elephant beach is all about water activities. Eleven girls = eleven different opinions about which activities to engage in. Make that ten. I was clear I wanted nothing more than to stroll on the beach. No banana boats or parasailing or rough and tumble adventures in the water for me. In other words, I am a big chicken. I collected two more chickens from the group to stroll with me. The rest of the gang went off on an undersea adventure.

Elephant Beach is very picturesque, with lots of driftwood and a thick green forest cover. I wish we had more time to stroll around and click pictures of the views. Again, my fellow chickens and I fell prey to the selfie syndrome and spent most of the time clicking pictures of each other. We also ate heartily at the tiny line of food stalls on the beach. Chaat, fresh-cut fruits, juice, Maggi noodles ... everything was available, and we ate everything!

The rest of the gang arrived looking hyper-excited. Every time I thought our group could not get any more excited, a new threshold was reached. They had finished an undersea walk and could not stop talking about the wonders on the ocean floor. It was lucky for them that some of us had not gone along. They had an audience to listen to all their exploits and escapades.

All this left them hungry, so they proceeded to wipe out the food at one of the stalls before we headed back to the mainland for the next program. What a bunch of locusts!

Attention Radhanagar Beach!

Ah, Radhanagar Beach! This beach will be etched in our collective memories as the place where we became international celebrities.

We reached Radhanagar Beach with the single-minded determination to accomplish our Speedo beachwear photoshoot. Everyone donned the purple dress and padded barefoot on the soft white sand with great speed. Everyone except Live Wire, our designated showstopper. She had a blue Speedo swimsuit.

The beach was beautiful and the sand was white and soft. We threw away our slippers and enjoyed the feeling of the soft and fluffy sand on the soles of our feet. Not for long, though. It was nearing sunset, the golden hour. We had so many photos to click. Also, I want to add that we made quite a sight — a bunch of women in similar swimsuits of a rich purple color, with one blue swimsuit thrown into the mix. We were definitely head-turners!

Striking a pose

We dug up all the photos we had shared on WhatsApp as 'potential ideas' for our photoshoot and executed them one by one.

For the first one, we all had to merely stand in line with Live Wire at the center. No biggie. We stood in line and looked around for someone to click the picture. The beach lifeguards were sitting close by. Again, we fell into the mindset of a group mafia — we did not care what anyone thought! Leader just marched up to the closest one and requested him to click our picture. He did not have the power to refuse. No one can refuse Leader. But the lifeguard's body language left little doubt that he was ever going to click another photo for us. We heard him.

For the next one, we found someone who looked like they wouldn't mind clicking a photo or ten. The brief was simple. We had to stand in a single line angled slightly to the left, and raise our right legs sideways to a height of two feet. This may be hard to visualize, but it makes for a great pose. The volunteer clicked the photo. I ran to him to check the quality of the picture. It is important to carry out a quality check lest we be disappointed later. Erm. Small problem. Apparently, the pose memo had reached only half the population. No one after Live Wire had raised their legs. The photo looked funny. Instructions were given again and the volunteer did his job. All good. We had a fabulous photo.

While some of us were trying to come up with the next pose, others did not stand around wasting time. Really, you have to hand it to this group to use each minute efficiently. Huddles of two or three girls got together and carried out their own mini photoshoots. When we collected all the photos from everyone's phone camera in a shared drive, I understood how truly efficient these girls are!

The next pose involved all of us sitting in a wide circle on the beach with our legs stretched out in front of us. Our feet formed a small circle at the center. There was a little confusion about where Live Wire should sit. There is no show stopper slot in a circle. She just picked a spot and sat. A minute after we had all assumed position, we realized a major flaw in the plan. Everyone was settled. Who was going to find a photographer?

I guess a group of color-coordinated and uniformly dressed women sitting in a circle on the beach was pretty uncommon. A young boy and girl were passing by, understood our predicament, and volunteered to click pictures for us. Bless them! The boy patiently clicked photos from various angles while the girl gave him instructions to ensure everyone was covered without random body parts being chopped off. Yaay! We had another lovely group photo for our collection!

And then it started

It was around this time that the mobbing started. A couple of older women travelers on the beach came up to us hesitantly and asked if they could get a photo with the group. *Oi! What?* We looked at each other. Weird. But we got over it quickly and agreed. We had ulterior motives. As soon as the women got their photo with us, they found themselves holding one of our cameras. They had to return the favor by clicking a photo for us. Ha! Two birds with one stone!

We just closed this deal when a young boy came up with a similar request. Ok, this was mega weird. We may be over forty, but we were still wary of having pictures taken with strange young boys no matter how cute they were. We told him we were ok with clicking pictures if he brought his family. The boy scooted and came back with a wife, a father, a mother, and an assortment of other people. Oh my! Many photos were taken and they returned the favor by clicking several group pictures for us. They even suggested some poses.

The saga continued. At least seven to eight groups of people walked up and requested pictures with our group. What was the draw? I guess it is rare to see such an enthusiastic bunch of obviously middle-aged women living life freely and having so much fun. We were role models now. Several women blessed us and wished us many more such fun trips. How sweet of them! We may have inspired some women to embark on such trips with their own tribes. I hope we have. I hope this story inspires many more.

It was quite an evening. After we wound up and changed, we called home to let our families know what had transpired. Who knows if there was some TV crew hiding in the bushes and filming our theatrics? Imagine if our clueless families woke up to sensational headlines such as:

11 Women in Purple Swimsuits Set Radhanagar Beach on Fire

Unprecedented Activity on Radhanagar Beach Increases Local Temperatures

Locals Throng Radhanagar Beach to Catch a Glimpse of Celebrities in Purple Swimsuits

There was no news item anywhere, but we can imagine how many WhatsApp groups must have received our group photos taken with various families. They must have shared and overshared the pictures with their friends and families. It is not every day that people get the chance to pose with eleven nubile young women in swimsuits.

Meanwhile, we are waiting for a call from Speedo's marketing team. I am sure the sales of this particular model of swimsuit have taken off. It is comfortable, the color is deep and rich, suited all our body types, and made all of us look good.

Speedo folks — if you are reading this, feel free to contact me using the information provided at the end of this book. We are available for promos, modeling, and other such assignments. You can even sponsor our next trip to Bali. We are happy to model your new range of swimsuits exclusively.

There is something about being married, having kids who are no longer babies, and reaching a certain stage in life, I guess. We are okay with letting our hair down and enjoying ourselves without guilt. This does not come easily to women. There is also something to be said about girl gang groups. It is very liberating. There is a totally different vibe and freedom in such groups, especially if we are lucky to find a like-minded tribe. Touch wood!

The key person

After a tiring photoshoot, we headed to the changing rooms on the beach. Button, Diva, and I walked down the road to drink a cup of well-earned chai. Suddenly there was some commotion among the other girls. We heard one word being repeated in a high pitch by Witty — *key, key, key*.

Witty and Ms. Coach were having an animated conversation about some key. Closer observation yielded the information that Witty's locker key was lost. She believed she had given it to Ms. Coach. Ms. Coach had no memory of this event and therefore, no key. The locker key at these beach locations is usually firmly tied to an elastic wristband. You simply wear the key on your wrist and forget all about it. It stays put while you have fun and come back. The system is flawless and ensures no one drops their key in the ocean. Ah, yes. But I guess we are above such fool-proof methods. We broke the system. Looking for this key on a vast sandy beach seemed worse than looking for a needle in a haystack. At least the haystack will end at some point. A sand-filled beach stretches to infinity.

The situation was tense. As Button, Diva, and I calmly sipped our tea, we watched the action unfold. The girls were looking for the lost key in various bags, on each others' wrists, pockets and what have you. As Diva raised her hand for another sip of tea, Button had a casual question for her.

"Hey, what's that on your wrist?"

Diva looked puzzled. It was an elastic wristband with a key on it. *Oh!*

Realization hit all three of us at the same moment. We ran to the other girls shouting *key, key, key*! It was the missing locker key belonging to Witty.

What will continue to remain missing is the information on how the key appeared on Diva's wrist. Neither Diva nor Witty had a clue about this mystery. Ms. Coach felt exonerated from the crime of having lost a key she never had in the first place. We may have found the key, but we feel we are still missing a key piece of information in this matter. Sadly, it will remain a mystery.

Dinner at Havelock

After a hectic day of dancing and grueling photoshoots amid the glare of public adoration, we were tired. We just wanted a quiet dinner and a warm bed. That did not prevent us from dressing up for dinner. The dresses we had packed needed airtime. Photos were going to be clicked at dinner too, of that we had not a shred of doubt.

What we did not know was our propensity to dance at any given point of night or day. We had danced for ages on the ferry in the morning and were hoping there would be no music at the resort that night. Sadly, there was. Sadly, the DJ was good. Sadly, he played amazing Bollywood dance numbers.

Our body parts began to move involuntarily because our brains were under the misguided impression that we were terribly tired. After a point, our brains got the message about our body parts being in motion. Signals were sent to allow our feet to take us to the dance floor. No one could resist the call of the dance floor. Food and drinks were forgotten as we did not want to miss a single '*this song is sooo good to dance to*' number.

We just could not stop dancing. In the end, the DJ had to ask us to evacuate the dance floor because he was too tired. Even the '*I have two left feet*' people were *bitten badly by the boogie bug*.

We earned our sleep that night. We had worked hard the whole day!

Our private beach at the resort

We had to leave early the next morning for Neil Island. We gulped down our breakfast at the Havelock Island Resort and headed down to the private access beach. It was deliciously beautiful. There was hardly anyone around. The colors of the sea, pebble-strewn sands, a few gracefully angled palms — everything looked like it had been put together by landscape artists. I guess it was, by the best artist of them all — nature. We just sat on the beach and drank in huge gulps of the serene beauty around us. The exquisiteness of the landscape and the gentle waves lapping at our feet washed over us and engulfed us in a warm embrace.

Eventually, we heard the all too familiar bugle call — *GIRRLLLSSSSS*! It was time to move on to the next adventure. We had the important task of setting other beaches on fire.

10

Next Stop, Neil Island

On day three, we reached Neil Island by ferry from Havelock Island. Our fellow passengers were lucky. We were offloaded before the music and dancing on the ferry started. We checked into TSG Aura and were herded off to the first port of call.

Kaftans krazies on Bharatpur Beach

Before we could say, "Look at the beach, it is so beautiful", two things happened.

- One bunch of girls spotted a few beachside shops selling shellware and beads and whatnot. Within ten minutes, efficient haggling happened and several sets of necklaces and bead chains traded hands. Some of our girls were so generous that they bought sets for all of us. I found myself stuffing my bag with the spoils of their battle with the stall owners.

- Princess and Leader had found a professional photographer for hire. A deal had been struck to click a few thousand photos of the group for a nominal cost. Princess was very smug about this coup. "Now we don't have to beg strangers to click our photos," she said clearly unhappy about our Radhanagar 'photographer hunting' experience.

We hit the beach with the hapless photographer. For the next hour, we hounded him with our ideas about poses and made him click several photos again because they were not up to the mark. Diva was our appointed quality officer. I guess, being the youngest, it helped that she has great eyesight. I, for one, could barely see the screen of the photographer's regular digital camera. The blinding light reflecting off the almost-white sands did not do much to improve visibility. Diva did her job to perfection. She pouted for the photos and sashayed to the camera to check with military precision. This was repeated almost a hundred times. When we left, we had about thirty-five Diva-approved photos loaded on all our phones.

This time we were all wearing our colorful kaftans over whatever was beneath them. That didn't matter. The kaftans were translucent, wispy, and fluttered delicately in the sea breeze, lending so much beauty to our photo-op. The solos and the group photos turned out to be picture-perfect. Something about the vast and underpopulated Bharatpur Beach, the blue-green sea gently lapping at our feet, and the weightlessness of no responsibilities such as kids and family liberated us, and all of us looked lovely without exception. In a different world, we could have been models — every single one of us. The photos are a visual and aesthetic treat and help us love ourselves no matter what shape or size we are.

Princess and Leader can take extra brownie points for finding and hiring a professional photographer. I suppose it helped that the background and the subjects were equally stunning!

Monkey menace at Natural Bridge

We dragged ourselves to the next destination — Natural Bridge. We had to climb a few steps up and then down to a rocky stretch of beach. Since it was low tide, we could walk on the dead corals and rocks on the beach to reach this amazing natural formation — a huge rock jutting out with a hole carved in the middle by the relentless battering of waves. Here again, our nature artist is at work to create spectacular landscapes.

Not everyone is adept at walking on rocks and uneven surfaces. While the rest scampered off to reach the bridge, Princess and I took it a little slow. I am a confirmed chicken. This time Princess decided to keep me company. By the time we reached the foot of the bridge, the troops had clambered atop and again bullied some passing tourists to click pictures. As the men happily obliged, we caught the women shouting at the men to hurry up. But hey, the men had an important task at hand. They weren't about to hurry!

Princess and I witnessed all the fracas, laughed, and decided to head back. It was going to be a long arduous journey for us. Midway through our trek, we heard familiar voices. One of the voices said, "Ooh, these people are still here. I thought they left long ago." Before we could find our footing, turn around, and check who was talking, the voices turned into flesh and blood and passed us in a whoosh. Our kaftans fluttered at the speed of their passage. We saw the backs of Live Wire and Earth Girl and realized it was Live Wire talking. Live Wire mumbled something about a bathroom emergency to explain their hurried departure. Sure, that made us feel better about how fast they blitzed past us!

Princess was miffed. Here we were, bravely struggling to get to the other side on slippery rocks and coral, while those two shot by as if walking on air. She was later heard reporting the matter to others in a huff, "They rushed past us like hungry monkeys." It *did* seem like that. How did they walk at that speed? When we reached the van pickup point, the two had eaten, drunk tea, showered, peed, changed their clothes, and maybe caught a short nap, too. They looked that fresh. Ugh, these active monkeys!

Earth Girl is lithe and light and agile and Live Wire is ... well, a live wire!

Sunset at Laxmanpur Beach

We boarded the van for the next stop. All that hard work had made us hungry. Ms. Coach dipped into her bottomless Coach bag and dug out candied fruits. She is such a confirmed fruitaholic that I wonder if she has fruits hidden in various parts of her clothing too, just in case there is a fruit emergency. It was an emergency on the van since we all felt dehydrated. She revived us with candied fruits, mouth fresheners, and nuts. That girl carries the entire planet in her bag. What a lifesaver!

A sweaty but happy bunch was offloaded by the van onto Laxmanpur Beach to enjoy the sunset.

Again, we were amazed at the clean beach, velvety sands, and turquoise waters. Some folks just flopped on the sand to gaze at the horizon. A bunch of us started walking along the shoreline with our feet grazing the water. It was glorious. The sands were teeming with life. We watched enthralled as hermit crabs carried their entire houses around on their backs. We ogled at the shells and rocks hewn into exotic shapes by the waves. We were mesmerized by the beauty of driftwood scattered aesthetically all over the beach — neither too much nor too little. It was a perfect arrangement that added oodles of character to the beach.

We were so engrossed in our silent walk that we did not notice the lack of a sunset. It was slightly cloudy, so the sunset was shrouded in mystery.

By the time we walked back to the van, Pataki informed us that her retirement plans were in place. Button and Pataki had a startup idea. They had even included Live Wire as an employee in their new business. They were both going to retire to Neil Island and run a business to promote local art and craft. Live Wire was recruited as she is multitalented. She can draw, crochet, stitch, make jewelry, and who knows what else. All this in the time some of us watch a show on TV.

Pataki had identified her target audience and location for the business as well. The location was Laxmanpur Beach and the target audience was slightly old men who could be convinced into buying crafts produced by local girls. Pataki's eyes were on fire as she rolled out the business plan to us. We huddled around her and lapped it all up. I will not be surprised to find her on the beaches of the Andaman Islands executing her brilliant game plan a few years from now. She is a woman with a lot of spunk.

We applauded Pataki and Button for their plan, wished them great success, and secretly hoped they would indeed succeed because we would have a home or two to stay at whenever we visited the Andamans. And visit again we will, we are so in love with the place.

While we were engrossed in the business plan unveiling ceremony, a sharp call of *GIRRLLSSSS* reached us in the dark evening air. We responded to the call by bleating and rushing towards our van.

Ruckus at dinner

Dinner at TSG Aura was wonderful. They gave us the entire first floor of the restaurant to ourselves. Someone must have pre-warned them about how loud and disruptive we could be. Having the entire floor served to make us noisier, if that is possible. Yes, of course it is possible.

I discovered one spot at our table where the lighting was perfect for portrait photos. I made everyone sit in that hot seat in turn and tried to click a lovely solo photo. While each person came and occupied the hot seat, others had a few things to do:

- Engage the hot seat person in conversation
- Make sure their head did not tilt too much
- Make sure they mostly listened and did not talk or move much
- Keep the conversation funny. We needed teeth to show in the form of a smile or laugh

Leader, Mom, and Live Wire learned these rules quickly and implemented them diligently for each hot seater! Overall it was fun and everyone loved their portraits or at least, they told me they did. Not that they had much choice after all the drama involved.

Talking through the night wearing *lotthe* clothes

After dinner, Leader had a single instruction for us. As our trip was almost coming to a close, we needed to gather and chat through the night. It was deemed mandatory. She said, "Girrrrlssss, wear '*lotthe*' clothes and gather in Room 1."

We were happy to comply. We wore our 'lotthee-est' clothes and crowded into Room 1.

It is hard to explain *lotthe* in English. It is a mix of casual, dull, worn-out, overused, sloppy, floppy, or something encompassing all this. If you know a single English word that can convey this, let me know.

One tiny two-person bedroom expanded magically to accommodate eleven exuberant girls set for a night of tittle-tattle. About six people somehow draped themselves all over the bed while the rest slumped on chairs, tables, and even the floor. A wide range of topics was covered. If anyone was seen falling asleep, their eyes were propped open with toothpicks. We continued talking and laughing late into the night.

Much later the next day, we realized something. The tour operator had given us one important piece of information about Neil Island which we had completely forgotten. Actually, let me be honest. We had not listened to him while he supplied this information. He had told us not to miss the night sky at Neil Island. It is supposed to be spectacular and one might even see the Milky Way. Neil Island is famous for astronomy tourism and people come from far and wide to stare up at the clear skies.

Ha! Missed. With all the chattering that had to be purged from our systems, where was the time to silently gaze up at the sky?

Sunrise at Neil Island

Despite being up late into the night, some of us were motivated enough to rise very early. Sunrise on the beach was a sight not to be missed. We were so glad we made the effort to rise and shine early. Considering there was a pristine beach two steps away from our rooms, it would have been criminal to miss the scene.

It was a morning well spent. There was something magical about standing on the beach as darkness turned to light. To watch the sun appear hesitantly at first, painting the sky and the waters in rich colors, and suddenly burst across the sky in all his dazzling brilliance was both mesmerizing and humbling at once.

Add trees, friendly dogs, intricately wave-carved driftwood, the beautiful play of light, the velvety sand, and clear blue waters to the mix — it was a heady cocktail. We felt drunk on nature's gift to us that morning — a show that we should pay for by treating the earth better, by living lightly, and by being grateful for the ability to see and experience such rich performances.

We returned to our rooms with our hearts brimming over with inexplicable joy.

Heading back to Port Blair

Back in our rooms, the mood had grown a bit somber. We had to leave this paradise and head back to civilization soon. We were busy getting ready in our rooms, listlessly picking up our things, and packing for the last leg of the journey. The mood was broken by a high-pitched scream. Actually, two screams rent the air. We rushed out of our rooms convinced something horrible had happened to one of us. Touch wood, all of us were fine.

Button and Pataki were busy chattering animatedly. Wait — who was who? Suddenly we were playing 'spot the six differences.' They were both wearing the exact same type of dress and looking terribly cute. Lesser mortals would have followed up the shrieks by running back to change to undo this fashion faux pas. Not Button and Pataki. They were reveling in the coincidence.

What are the chances, I ask you, that two people who live across town from each other went shopping unbeknownst to each other and bought the exact same dress? What are the chances that out of five action-packed days involving multiple opportunities to change clothes, they both chose this morning to wear this dress?

And Lord Almighty, tell us, what are the chances that they are both petite and cute and look like twins?

It was all too much to handle. Naturally, the big reveal was followed by a half-hour huddle on how, what, who, where, when, and so on until all mysteries were solved in our collective minds. The crowd named them Chungu-Mungu and dispersed to get ready. Our spirits were lifted by this strange occurrence.

Chung-Mungu were obviously dressed and ready to leave and became eagerly available for a twin photo shoot. I was totally carried away by the flexibility and enthusiasm of my two petite models. They stood where I said they should, assumed whatever pose I asked them to, and participated so wholeheartedly that I began to see why people make a career out of photography. It was addictive. My models were like two little fluffballs oozing cuteness.

On that note of daintiness overload, we bid adieu to the beautiful Neil Island.

11

Heaviness at the Cellular Jail

Compared to the rest of the trip, the visit to the Cellular Jail put us in a very different mood.

It should not take us a visit to historical landmarks to handle our freedom with the respect it deserves. As a nation, we are rejoicing and leading our lives the way we want based on the heroic struggles of our ancestors — thousands of nameless people who laid down their lives so we can live and breathe freely.

Sometimes, we forget.

That's when a trip down our history lane helps. No trip to the Andamans is complete without a visit to the famous Cellular Jail or Kala Pani. Kala Pani — dark waters or the end of life surrounded by water? Either way, it feels dark and foreboding.

The Andaman Islands were used as a place to exile political prisoners of the Indian freedom struggle. The Cellular Jail was built by the British in the Andamans between 1896 and 1906 to house convicts and freedom fighters.

The building with a central tower and seven arms stretching out is an architectural marvel. A single guard in the central tower could keep an eye on the entire jail that could house more than 700 prisoners at a time. We didn't really need that architectural marvel to be built on the graves of so many Indians. But it is there. And it serves as a huge memory of their sacrifice.

We clicked a few group photos outside the building. Then we stepped in. Selfies and group photos were forgotten. Everything else was forgotten. A sense of heaviness descended upon us. There was something in the very air. As Ms. Coach said, "It feels like the spirits of the freedom fighters are still here."

Unexpectedly, we found ourselves on the brink of tears. One look at some of the depictions of torture and the devices used was enough to tip us over. I could not contain the deep sense of sorrow that engulfed me. I rushed out of the museum room to find Button and Ms. Coach in the same state — crying copiously. The stories were overwhelming.

Meanwhile, others wanted details. They wanted to know as much as they could so as to understand and feel. We hired a guide to help us with more information. The passion with which he explained everything struck a chord within us. This was no ordinary guide just doing his job — he was someone who knew a lot, felt deeply, and wanted to communicate that feeling to his audience.

However, his empathetic explanation only served to make it worse for a few of us. We decided to skip the next couple of stops — the oil mill and the gallows. The oil mill is where our freedom fighters were beaten and flogged mercilessly while they rotated the machinery to generate coconut oil. Enough said. We did not need to see the models to visualize the barbarism. The entrance to the oil mill looks so pretty set against the blue sky and surrounded by lush greenery. We could be forgiven for being swayed by the beauty and peace of the place. Luckily, the heaviness in the air prevented us from forgetting.

Our next stop in the guided tour was the cells where the inmates were housed — imprisoned for the horrible crime of wanting to be free. Imagine wanting freedom! So they were incarcerated in tiny, identical cells and were moved around periodically to disorient them and prevent any long-term recognition that might help them escape. Escape indeed! What awaited them outside the cellular jail was the deep, blue sea. Where would they swim off to?

We heard from the guide that the cells in each tower were built in such a way that the entrance of one block faced the back of the next. There was no way for the inmates to communicate.

I could go on. But only a visit and listening to some of the stories will make anyone understand the feelings the place evokes. When a couple of us were huddled outside the oil mill waiting for the others, the guide joined us. He said he sensed how deeply we felt. He talked about how he watches the eyes of the people gathered around him when he narrates his stories. "The eyes reveal whether they are genuinely interested or just drifting along," he said. Our eyes were wet. He smiled knowingly.

None of us in our group clicked a single selfie. That's saying something for a group of eleven photo-crazy women. We were all humbled, the scale of the sacrifices weighing heavily on us. Who were these people? What were they made of? How did they stay motivated in a place like this with inhuman treatment from their fellow humans? What drives humans to treat other humans in such a ruthless manner?

So many questions. The only answer, loud and clear:

Do not take your freedom lightly!

12

Magical Ross Island

After the heavy experience at the Cellular Jail, we headed to Ross Island by ferry.

Subhas Chandra Bose Island, formerly known as Ross Island, was our last stop. It was worth every minute spent on the island. I'd say it was complete *paisa vasool* for me — meaning, I got my entire money's worth in the two-hour window spent on that island. Now I am left thirsting for more.

We hopped on a ferry for an approximately 10-minute ride from Port Blair to Ross Island. We jumped off the ferry and into a strange world — a world where deer roamed free, where the forest had reclaimed the space that belonged to it, and where palms held their heads high and watched over us like sentinels of the island.

The first gasp from me was when I sighted all those deer. The place was teeming with spotted deer and all of them seemed utterly friendly. Some of them looked like they wanted to strike up a conversation with us.

After meeting and greeting some of those cute fellas, we hired a buggy to drive us around the island. We were on a tight schedule. We had to gather at a designated location in an hour for the famous light and sound show.

The buggy ride was fun. The drivers doubled up as guides and pointed to landmarks all over the island. They talked about how Ross Island was ravaged by the Japanese during the Second World War, by an earthquake, and by the tsunami of 2004. In spite of repeated attacks by humans and nature, Ross Island stands proud and bears witness to all that it has seen and endured.

As we drove uphill in the buggy, I exclaimed often and begged the buggy driver to stop for me to click photos. I was not above jumping off the moving buggy to capture all that I could. The whole thing felt rushed. I wish we had more time. There were so many ruins of old British and Japanese buildings. They looked beautiful with the vines and tree branches that had grown all over them. Reclamation — the forest winning over man-made structures. What a sight it was!

The ride uphill was dotted with a generous sprinkling of spotted deer. I tried to talk to them and even addressed a baby as Bambi. That cracked up my buggy driver. Bambi seemed to like the name too. He actually looked up when I called out!

We arrived at the top of the hill. Our buggy driver told us we had twenty minutes to visit the lighthouse and get back to the buggy. I am telling you now — twenty minutes was absolutely not enough! Arrive early on the island. Reach the top of the hill faster. Do something, anything! But make sure you have more time to walk down to the lighthouse and back. Seriously!

We walked down a series of steps and caught our breaths often as we descended towards the sea. The palms at artistic angles, the rays of the 'getting ready to set' sun streaming through the trees, the glorious colors of the sea, and that impossibly stunning lighthouse! I was overcome by the beauty all around us.

We could not walk up to the lighthouse — instead, we had to stop at a small viewing platform. I settled down there, staring out into the sea, enjoying the gusty sea breeze, wondering about the lives of the sailors, the British officers, the prisoners who were brought to the island, our freedom fighters, and so on. It was a heavy and heady moment rolled into one.

Just when I thought Ross Island couldn't get any better, there was a deafening roar in the sky. Two Indian Air Force fighter jets streaked through the sky, one from the right and another from the left. They criss-crossed each other above my head and sped away into the horizon. I screamed with the sheer excitement of hearing that high-decibel roar, the speed with which the jets cut through the sky, and the unbelievable coincidence of being at that exact spot at that moment in time. It is hard to capture my emotion in words. I thought I would explode with the sheer joy and excitement of it all.

Sitting there at the tip of the island and watching our fighter pilots in action preparing for an aero show filled my heart with pride. Our own real-life *mavericks* were in the air, superbly manning their fabulous aircraft, and guarding our skies. Having heard the heart-rending stories of our freedom struggle earlier in the afternoon, the sight of India's defense prowess on display re-ignited our spirit of patriotism.

Everything looked amazing. Everything felt right.

Reluctantly, led by the rays of the setting sun, we returned to our buggy and rode down to watch the light and sound show. Apparently, Ross Island has no dearth of ideas on 'how to wow an innocent tourist.'

While we waited for the show to begin, one of the guides on the island came along and told us that there were 550 deer on the island. We learned that the lady is a self-appointed guardian for the island's varied fauna such as deer, squirrels, bulbuls, eagles, and so on. Someone told us that she is a squirrel whisperer and had named a lot of the island's squirrels. She calls them by name and they respond with the same level of enthusiasm and love that she showers on them. It was amazing to meet someone like her.

The light and sound show was spectacular. Sitting under a clear black sky dotted with countless stars, we listened to the narration of the Indian freedom struggle and all that was endured in the Andaman Islands. We were again reminded of how precious our freedom is.

Too soon, it was time to leave. No one is allowed to stay on Ross Island, and thank heavens for that. The island remains clean and un-touristified!

Ross Island left me breathless. I need more time on that island. I need to spend time staring at the ruins and at the creeper-like trees. I need to stop and chat with the deer. I need to meet the squirrel whisperer. I need to sit down and stare at the vast sea and the beacon of light.

I'll be back, Ross Island!

13

A Party Fit for a Princess

After a heavy and heady day at the Cellular Jail and Ross island, we should have been tired and dropped dead as soon as we reached the hotel at Port Blair. Right? Nonsense! You should know us better by now.

It was our last day in town. Tomorrow, we were going to head back to reality. All we wanted was to let our hair down and party. We had a very valid excuse to party, we had a birthday baby on board — our Princess. A few of us had already plotted together and managed to organize a cake. We also had a killer venue for the celebration — a rooftop bar and restaurant. Princess was oblivious to our stealth planning. We hoped.

Leader and I tried to make reservations. We were a big gang. It might be hard to get a table later, right? But the hotel refused. It was Saturday night. 'Walk in and check if you are lucky' night!

We dressed hurriedly and reached the rooftop restaurant in record time. Leader was trying to keep the cake a secret. She asked me to take the troops upstairs while she followed us with the cake. I was ecstatic. I was now in command. Buoyed by all that we had heard about freedom·fighters, I marched the troops up and requested a table for eleven.

The maître d'hôtel refused. He said they were up to their eyeballs with guests or something like that. I persisted. I told him one of us was a birthday baby and it would be great to celebrate at a place with such a lovely vibe. His face said, "As if I haven't heard that excuse earlier."

He bowed low, put his hand on his chest, and was on the verge of tears as he said he was helpless but there was really no room for such a big crowd. What a show he put on — I almost gave him an Oscar. He was right, though. The place with spilling people from the tables into the walking pathways. I slow-marched the disappointed troops back to the ground floor. I informed Leader and told her we should just go to the restaurant and order.

Leader would have none of it. She was not used to such treatment. *No* was not in her vocabulary. She asked me to hold my horses and marched up. 3 minutes later, she called and asked me to round up the troops. We had a table. What is this woman made of? I saw the place. It was packed. What did she do? How does she work such magic each time? When we went back up, some folks hurriedly vacated a nearby table, and it became our home for the rest of the lovely evening. I am glad Leader is on our side. I'd be worried if I were the maître d'.

The clear sky, crisp air, and the overall mood of the place turned us into a happy lot. I am not saying the drinks didn't help. I was using eye contact with Leader and a few other people who knew the secret to communicate when to pull out the carefully concealed cake. Meanwhile, a loud voice interrupted.

"Heyy! When is the cake cutting?"

We were all thrown. It was supposed to be a secret! But Princess was sitting there with a naughty and knowing smile, clearly struggling to look surprised. No Oscar for her performance. She said she had somehow figured out we had organized a cake. We were a leaky boat apparently! Bah! So much for keeping secrets.

The great reveal before time did not dampen our spirits. We drank, cut cake, sang lustily for Princess, called her husband and made him wish her, and created a grand ruckus befitting a true princess. Amid teary-eyed speeches and multiple thank yous from the obviously touched Princess, Leader called our van and ordered us to head home. *GIRRRLLLSSSSSS*! We bleated and followed.

I don't think Leader will ever trust me again with any responsibility. I had one job — getting a table. Oh, how I had failed! I cried myself to sleep that night.

14

All Good Things Must Come to an End

Just like that, five days had whooshed past us. It was time to head home.

But first, a spot of shopping

That's right — just a *spot* of shopping. We had very little time left to reach the airport. Our van drove us from the hotel straight to the shopping area, where there was a shop filled with all kinds of local jewelry. The girls became homing pigeons.

I was not terribly inclined to shop. Instead, I reclined in the van and watched life go by. Mom was with me. We used the time gainfully to ensure all expenses had been accounted for on our trusted app, Splitwise. The app took away the burden of hanging on to bills and keeping track of who paid for what. Apps like this are life savers on multi-people trips. No one remembers details about who paid for the chai at one beach or peanuts at another. The app keeps track of it all, does the complex math, and tells us who needs to pay whom and how much. At the end of the trip, for some reason, I owed Witty Rs. 9.09. She was sure she had never paid for a single thing the entire trip. I took her word for it. I did not pay her back on the grounds that I cannot pay back something that has not been paid for in the first place. We both gained international fame for our constant bickering.

Pro tip: Make sure the entire group downloads one single app to help split all expenses. Make entries as you spend so as to not lose track. Or you could appoint one person to do the needful. In our case, I was the appointee. I was given a name for this activity. *Muniamma*.

Here's the etymology for the name *Muniamma:*

In Hindi, 'munim' is the term used to refer to the bookkeeper in small businesses. The job is usually associated with a male. Since I am a woman, we came up with *Muniamma*. When anyone paid for something, they just summoned Muniamma and made sure the bookkeeping was in order.

But I digress. Mom and I finished checking the app, chatted about this and that, checked our messages, called home, ate some snacks, tapped our feet restlessly, and yet there was no sign of the shoppers. When they finally emerged from the shop, their hands were filled with heavy bags. They were bursting with excitement and could not wait to show Mom and I the fruit of their labor over the past hour.

Meanwhile, I was looking out of the window and noticed the owners closing the shop. They displayed a board saying '**Out of Stock. Will re-open next month**.' and went home. My, our girls are such power shoppers!

You can shop at airports too

We reached the airport, checked in, and settled down to wait for our flight. I went to the bathroom and came back to find just one or two of our group in the waiting area. Where did the others disappear? Why was no one panicking?

The girls had spotted a lone shop at the airport. It sold jewelry. Oh my! The girls had launched themselves at the shop like a swarm of bees buzzing around a beehive. You would think they had had no chance to shop at Port Blair at all. They came back excited, cheeks flushed, hands full of goodies as if they had won the World Cup. I am not complaining. Earth Girl had magicked a pair of beautiful pearl earrings for all of us from the shop. It was love at first sight for me. I wear those pearls often now.

Our return flight was uneventful and un-chatterful, which is saying something. We were wistful and exhausted. Except, strangely, Pataki who normally does not talk much. She sat next to her twin, Button, and talked non-stop. In her own words, she later told Button, "I am sorry I did not let you close your eyes by keeping my mouth open at all times."

The cab ride back home

So much loot was collected because of all the gift-giving during the trip. I am a collector. I brought home a cute tub of cold cream, a brilliant yellow-blue necklace and earring set made of shell, a charcoal-infused soap, a beautiful blue stone necklace, a charming pair of pearl earrings, a billion photos, truckloads of love, and fabulous memories.

Ms Coach, Pataki, and I were headed home in a single cab. The mood was mellow. We were going to be accosted by reality after five days of living in fantasy land. Our cab driver was a kind man. He caught the mood and engaged us in pleasant conversation about the trip.

Finally, he made a statement that bathed us in a delicious, warm sensation. He said,

> "No matter where you go in the world, when you enter Bangalore, have fresh, fluffy idlis, hot filter coffee, and listen to a song by Annavru (actor late Dr. Rajkumar), you are home!"

We were home! Ready for the next adventure!

15

Post-trip Hubbub

The hangover lasted for a whole week — two days longer than the duration of the trip. We were tripping on the trip for a long time. For starters, photos and videos from all our cameras had to be consolidated. That took some work. I created a couple of Google albums to enable everyone to share their photos in a single place.

Pro tip: Just create one common photo album. Don't use too much energy to create multiple albums to cleanly separate people, scenery, and various destinations. People mix things up. I found more people in the scenery album than in the people album.

The group spent a lot of time post-trip going through the gazillion photos, re-posting them on our WhatsApp group, commenting on them, and analyzing them.

We had settled all accounts at the airport before leaving Port Blair, but Live Wire was still rather unsettled. She had this nagging feeling that she owed someone something more. After we got home, she somehow worked on the entire math manually and produced a report that proved she owed a couple of people. She paid them and finally slept peacefully that night, I suppose.

Next up was a bunch of heartfelt thank you notes on the group chat. Everyone thanked everyone else profusely. Seriously though — it was such a group effort to pull off a trip like this without a single hitch!

Recruitment will open shortly to fill a spot to make our group a dirty dozen. Terms and conditions apply.

Lastly, we have initiated an important conversation about our next destination. Stay tuned!

16

Addendum: Travel Tips for Girl Gangs

Pro tip collection center

All pro tips sprinkled across chapters in this book have been collected here for easy access:

Pro tip: For every girl gang trip, there has to be one designated leader. The rest of the gang must submit and emulate sheep. Where the leader goes, we simply follow. Ours not to reason why. Ours just to bleat and follow. There was one designated leader for the Maldives trip, too. It was a successful model. We simply replicated the process with a new leader. And boy, did she lead! It is not easy to herd ten wayward, 'head in the clouds' girls through a trip with a tight schedule. But Leader managed. We missed no sight and left no one behind! Her battle cry? *GIRRLLSSSSSS!*

That's all it took to round us all up over WhatsApp and later on the trip.

Pro tip: When you plan a girl gang trip, make sure every member of the group is equally interested in photos — both posing for and taking photos. Your recruitment strategy for the girl gang must lend extreme importance to this aspect. It is a deal breaker. In our group of eleven, even if one of us had been photo averse, it would have rained on the parade. Every last one of us is photo crazy. We will pose for group photos and solos with equal enthusiasm.

Pro tip: If you are planning a trip with your girl gang, do take the time to peruse the daily schedule in advance. See if you can cut down on some activities, prune the schedule a bit, and so on. Or leave it all to the trip leader and indulge in a shot of *que sera sera*. Whatever will be, will be. We did just that and it all worked out fine.

Pro tip: When ordering lunch or dinner for a big group, hand total control over to one person, or two, at max. Trust them to make the right choices, and then proceed to quietly eat whatever they ordered. If you are unhappy with their choices, take over the reins the next time.

Pro tip: Make sure the entire group downloads one single app to help split all expenses. Make entries as you spend so as to not lose track. Or you could appoint one person to do the needful. In our case, I was the appointee. I was given a name for this activity. *Muniamma*.

Pro tip: Just create one common photo album. Don't use too much energy to create multiple albums to cleanly separate people, scenery, and various destinations. People mix things up. I found more people in the scenery album than in the people album.

Bonus: whom to pack on a girl gang trip

Pack a doctor

This is critical. We had two — a dentist and a gynecologist. Several important body parts were covered because of these two talented people. Even a small sniffle brought the two rushing to attend to us. We felt safe and taken care of.

Definitely pack a fruitaholic

Have at least one fruit-crazy girl. She will buy fruits, stock up on fruits, and supply fruits to everyone throughout the trip.

Pack accessory collectors and distributors

Who knows what will come in handy for whom. Button was so well-accessorized at all times. I lost track of what she supplied to others throughout the trip.

I had worn a nice, deep blue dress for the grand dinner party, but I had nothing on my hands other than a finger ring. Live Wire who was ready in seconds as usual, was carrying out an inspection of all rooms to see how the 'getting ready' was progressing. She looked at me, told me my dress was lovely, and asked,

"Why are your hands naked?"

"Erm, because this dress has no sleeves," I said.

Live Wire immediately took off the watch she was wearing and ordered me to wear it.

It was the perfect shade of deep blue to go with my dress. Unbelievable. I was mesmerized by the magic a girl gang can produce on a trip. I accepted her offer and wore the watch proudly for the evening. I was even tempted to *forget* to return the watch because I knew I wouldn't find an accessory that matched my dress so perfectly even if I went hunting for it.

Several such accessory-swapping events dotted the trip. I cannot fathom how these girls can pack so many necklaces, watches, clothes, footwear, and what have yous in a small suitcase.

Pack a photographer

I am the self-appointed photographer for this gang. I enjoy making pictures and seeing happy faces when they see lovely pictures of themselves. You must pack one such person because photography is a critical requirement on all women's trips. Do not underestimate the importance of a photographer for girl gang outings. Or you could find yourself a girl gang that abhors photos. Yeah — good luck with that!

Pack a hat carrier

Everyone carries hats on beach trips. But pack one person who owns one big hat. It comes in handy as a prop for some fabulous photo opportunities. Diva is our official hat carrier. This is so well known that when she lost her lovely hat at one of the beaches, the universe quickly conspired and made an equally stunning hat available in the van as soon as she climbed in. Not kidding!

Pack some chatterboxes

Ah, right! That's pretty much everyone actually!

Pack a listener

When you have a gang of babbling babes, you need at least one person to listen to whatever is going on. We have Earth Girl. She misses nothing and listens with utmost attention to everything everyone says. When she comments on our WhatsApp group or in person, you get the sense that she has keenly observed, included deep thought, and provided a distilled opinion.

Pack someone with a sense of direction

Luckily, this was not in short supply for us. I, for one, am totally directionally challenged. It helps to have girls with a good sense of which way the hotel is. Definitely pack someone with a good sense of direction.

Most important ingredient to pack

Regardless of whether you pack clothes, shoes, or anything else, the one thing to definitely pack is your spirit of fun and adventure. You can milk the most out of even the shortest girl gang trip if you are high on enthusiasm and the will to have the time of your life!

Acknowledgments

There would be no story to tell without the group of friends who went on this wonderful trip.

I'd like to dedicate this book to my precious set of girlfriends from and *because of* school. Because of? Because they married my classmates from school. This is the best thing ever to have happened. My classmates who are boys could not have picked more perfect life partners for themselves, and in doing so, set in motion a chain of human relationships that will definitely withstand the test of time. Our lunch dates, discussions, festivals, and mega trips are tons of fun because everyone loves everyone else unconditionally. We have each others' backs at all times. Touch wood to this group and may we never have the evil eye on us.

I must thank a few people who gave me feedback on an early draft. In no particular order, Meghna, Asha, and Lakshmi for casting their eyes through the work-in-progress and giving me the conviction needed to take this story to completion.

Thank you to Samyuktha from Paper Lantern for a thorough review. I feel braver now to allow these pages to be seen by other eyes. Another thank you to Samyuktha for understanding the spirit of the book and helping design the super cute cover.

Afterword - Did You Enjoy This Story?

If you are here reading this page, I hope you read the rest of the book and enjoyed it.

If you purchased this book on Amazon, I'd like to make a request to you, dear reader, to leave a review for the book. Bonafide reviews go a long way in helping Amazon place this book in front of readers with similar reading tastes as yours.

Printed by Libri Plureos GmbH in Hamburg,
Germany